I SPY A FREIGHT TRAIN

— Transportation In Art —

For Walter and Molly

FOREWORD

You don't need to have any knowledge of art to introduce a child to a painting. You don't even need to know the name of the artist. All that is important is there in front of you in the picture, waiting to be discovered. Children love to look for details and will probably spot them before you do—the broken jug, the bird in the tree, the funny fish. You could talk about what the people are doing and what they're wearing, think about the time of year, the shapes and the colors and contrasts. Is it a quiet painting or a noisy one? Does it make you feel happy or sad? Is it old-fashioned or modern? Does it make you laugh? Could you copy it?

The children who helped me choose this small selection of paintings showed little interest in the artists, but they know the paintings inside out and will, I'm sure, remember them. I hope that the children sharing this book with you will enjoy the paintings as much as we have.

Lucy Micklethwait, 1996

I SPY
A
FREIGHT TRAIN

— Transportation In Art —

Devised & selected by Lucy Micklethwait

Greenwillow Books, New York

I spy
with my little eye

a car

Mel Ramos, *Batmobile*

I spy
with my little eye

a ship

Edward Burra, *The Annunciation, or St. Anne, St. Agnes and St. John Zachary*

I spy
with my little eye

an airplane

Eduardo Paolozzi, *Wittgenstein at the Cinema Admires Betty Grable*

Wittgenstein was always exhausted by his lectures. He was also revolted by them. He felt disgusted with what he had said and with himself. Often he would rush off to a cinema immediately after the class ended. As the members of the class began to move their chairs out of the room he might look imploringly at a friend and say in a low tone, 'Could you go to a flick?' On the way to the cinema Wittgenstein would buy a bun or cold pork pie and munch it while he watched the film. He insisted on sitting in the very first row of seats, so that the screen would occupy his entire field of vision, and his mind would be turned away from the thoughts of the lecture and his feelings of revulsion. Once he whispered to me, 'This is like a shower bath!' His observation of the film was not relaxed or detached. He leaned tensely forward in his seat and rarely took his eyes off the screen. He hardly ever uttered comments on the episodes of the film and did not like his companion to do so. He wanted to become totally absorbed in the film no matter how trivial or artificial it was, in order to free his mind temporarily from the philosophical thoughts that tortured and exhausted him. He liked American films and detested English ones. He was inclined to think that there could not be a decent English film. This was connected with a great distaste he had for English culture and mental habits in general. He was fond of the films starring Carmen Miranda and Betty Hutton. Before he came to visit me in America he demanded to me that I should introduce him to Miss Hutton.

Eduardo Paolozzi MARCH 1965

I spy
with my little eye

a horse

I spy
with my little eye

a rowboat

Wassily Kandinsky, *Birds*

I spy
with my little eye

a sleigh

Hendrick Avercamp, *A Winter Scene with Skaters near a Castle*

I spy
with my little eye

a wagon

I spy
with my little eye

a camel

Salvador Dali, *La Table Solaire*

I spy
with my little eye

a bicycle

Wayne Thiebaud, *Down Eighteenth Street (Corner Apartments)*

I spy
with my little eye

a freight
train

I spy
with my little eye

an elephant

Indian, *The Siege of Ranthambore*

I spy
with my little eye

a hot-air
balloon

Roger de la Fresnaye, *The Conquest of the Air*

I spy
with my little eye

a baby
carriage

What do you spy?

Richard Eurich, *Gay Lane*

I Spied with My Little Eye . . .

car
Mel Ramos (born 1935), *Batmobile* (1962)
Museum Moderner Kunst, Vienna, Bequest of the Austrian Ludwig Foundation

ship
Edward Burra (1905–1976), *The Annunciation, or St. Anne, St. Agnes and St. John Zachary* (1923)
Private Collection

airplane
Eduardo Paolozzi (born 1924), *Wittgenstein at the Cinema Admires Betty Grable* (1965) from *As Is When* (1964–1965)
The Tate Gallery, London

horse
Stanley Spencer (1891–1959), *Map Reading* (1932)
Sandham Memorial Chapel, Burghclere, Hampshire, The National Trust

rowboat
Wassily Kandinsky (1866–1944), *Birds* (1916)
Centre Georges Pompidou, Paris

sleigh
Hendrick Avercamp (1585–1634), *A Winter Scene with Skaters near a Castle* (about 1609)
The National Gallery, London

wagon
Vincent Van Gogh (1853–1890), *The Langlois Drawbridge* (1888)
Rijksmuseum Kröller-Müller, Otterlo

camel
Salvador Dali (1904–1989), *La Table Solaire* (1936)
Museum Boymans-van Beuningen, Rotterdam

bicycle
Wayne Thiebaud (born 1920), *Down Eighteenth Street
(Corner Apartments)* (1980)
Hirshhorn Museum and Sculpture Garden, Smithsonian Institution, Washington, D.C.,
Museum purchase with funds donated by Edward R. Downe, Jr., 1980

freight train
Ernst Thoms (1896–1938), *Train* (1926)
Kunstammlung der Stadtsparkasse, Hannover

elephant
Indian, *The Siege of Ranthambore* from *The Akbarnama* (about 1590)
The Victoria and Albert Museum, London

hot-air balloon
Roger de la Fresnaye (1885–1925), *The Conquest of the Air* (1913)
The Museum of Modern Art, New York, Mrs. Simon Guggenheim Fund

baby carriage
Richard Eurich (1903–1992), *Gay Lane* (1952)
Bradford Art Galleries and Museums, West Yorkshire

ACKNOWLEDGMENTS

The author and publishers would like to thank the galleries, museums, private collectors,
and copyright holders who have given their permission to reproduce the pictures in this book.

Mel Ramos, *Batmobile*, © Mel Ramos/DACS, London/VAGA, New York 1996.
Batman, Robin, and the Batmobile are trademarked
and copyrighted © DC Comics. Used with permission.

Edward Burra, *The Annunciation, or St. Anne, St. Agnes and St. John Zachary*.
Photograph courtesy of the Lefevre Gallery, London.

Eduardo Paolozzi, *Wittgenstein at the Cinema Admires Betty Grable*, © Eduardo Paolozzi

Stanley Spencer, *Map Reading*, © Estate of Stanley Spencer 1996. All rights reserved DACS.
Photograph courtesy of the National Trust Photographic Library.

Wassily Kandinsky, *Birds*, © ADAGP, Paris and DACS, London 1996.
Photograph Philippe Migeat © Centre Georges Pompidou.

Hendrick Avercamp, *A Winter Scene with Skaters near a Castle*,
reproduced by courtesy of the Trustees, The National Gallery, London.

Salvador Dali, *La Table Solaire*, © Demart Pro Arte BV/DACS 1996.

Wayne Thiebaud, *Down Eighteenth Street (Corner Apartments)*, © Wayne Thiebaud.
Photography by Ricardo Blanc.

Indian, *The Siege of Ranthambore* from *The Akbarnama*,
courtesy of the Board of Trustees of the Victoria and Albert Museum.

Roger de la Fresnaye, *The Conquest of the Air*.
Photograph © The Museum of Modern Art, New York.

Richard Eurich, *Gay Lane*, © Richard Eurich.

Cover picture: Ernst Thoms, *Train* (1926).
Title page picture: Vincent Van Gogh, *The Langlois Drawbridge* (1888).

Compilation and text copyright © 1996 by Lucy Micklethwait
The author asserts the moral right to be identified as the author of the work.
First published in Great Britain in 1996 by HarperCollins Publishers Ltd.
First published in the United States in 1996 by Greenwillow Books.
All rights reserved. No part of this book may be reproduced or utilized in any form or by any means,
electronic or mechanical, including photocopying, recording, or by any information storage and
retrieval system, without permission in writing from the Publisher, Greenwillow Books, a division
of William Morrow & Company, Inc., 1350 Avenue of the Americas, New York, NY 10019.
Printed in Hong Kong
First American Edition 10 9 8 7 6 5 4 3 2 1

Library of Congress Cataloging-in-Publication Data
Micklethwait, Lucy.
I spy a freight train: transportation in art /
selected and devised by Lucy Micklethwait.—1st American ed.
p.   cm.
Summary: Draws the viewer's eye to notice a transportation-related
object in each of the well-known paintings represented in this work.
ISBN 0-688-14700-3 (trade).   ISBN 0-688-14701-1 (lib. bdg.)
1. Transportation in art—Juvenile literature.   2. Art—Juvenile literature.
[1. Transportation in art.   2. Art appreciation.]
I. Title.   N8253.T68M53   1996
758'.9388—dc20   95-21429   CIP   AC